Thomas the Doubting Disciple

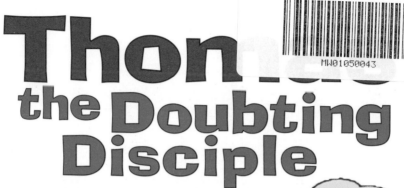

John 20:19–29 for Children

Written by Robert Baden
Illustrated by Andy Willman

Arch® Books
Copyright © 1997 Concordia Publishing House
3558 S. Jefferson Avenue, St. Louis, MO 63118-3968
Manufactured in Colombia

When Jesus rose on Easter Day,
His friends who saw Him said
To those who hadn't seen Him yet,
"Our Master is not dead!"

Those who had not seen Jesus knew
The others would not lie;
But it was so hard to believe,
For they had seen Him die.

So some believed, and some did not;
They weren't sure who was right.
To find the truth they said, "Let's meet
And talk this very night."

They found a room; they locked the door.
One thing they surely knew:
The evil ones who killed their Lord
Would like to kill them too!

They questioned, argued, thought, and talked.
They wondered what to do.
When suddenly they looked and saw
That Jesus stood there too!

They rubbed their eyes, they stared at Him.
Some laughed with joy; some cried,
"Oh, Jesus, is it really You?
We know for sure You died!"

He smiled and said, "Peace to you all.
Now look, all you who doubted."
They saw His nail-marked hands and feet.
"You *are* alive!" they shouted.

They talked about what had occurred
Till well into the night.
Then Jesus blessed them once again
And vanished from their sight.

Since Thomas, one of Jesus' friends,
Had missed his Master's visit,
The others cried, "He lives! It's true."
But Thomas just said, "Is it?

"Unless I see and touch His wounds
Made by the nails and spear,
I won't believe what you have said.
It's not enough to *hear*."

The following week, with Thomas there,
They met and locked the door.
And once again the Lord appeared
Just as He had before.

He blessed them, came to Thomas, showed
His wounds to him, and said,
"I know that for yourself you need
To *see* that I'm not dead.

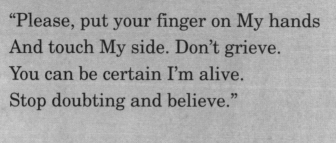

"Please, put your finger on My hands
And touch My side. Don't grieve.
You can be certain I'm alive.
Stop doubting and believe."

Thomas' heart was filled with joy
When he heard his Master's words;
He bowed his head, knelt down, and said,
"My risen God and Lord!"

"Dear Thomas," Jesus gently said,
"It's good what you've expressed.
You had to see Me to believe,
For you that was the best.

"But what you've seen today, all others
Must by faith receive.
And greatly blessed are those who haven't
Seen and yet believe."

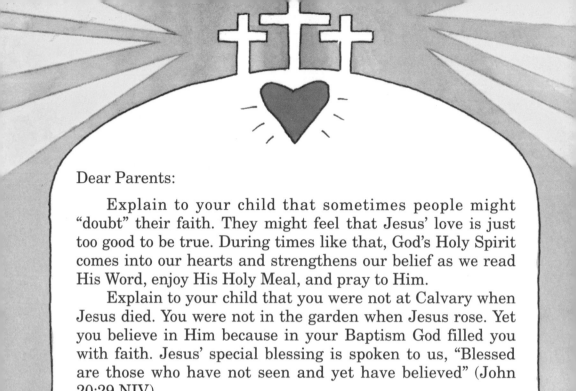

Dear Parents:

Explain to your child that sometimes people might "doubt" their faith. They might feel that Jesus' love is just too good to be true. During times like that, God's Holy Spirit comes into our hearts and strengthens our belief as we read His Word, enjoy His Holy Meal, and pray to Him.

Explain to your child that you were not at Calvary when Jesus died. You were not in the garden when Jesus rose. Yet you believe in Him because in your Baptism God filled you with faith. Jesus' special blessing is spoken to us, "Blessed are those who have not seen and yet have believed" (John 20:29 NIV).

Celebrate your sure faith in Jesus' resurrection with your child.

The Editor